Original title:
The Laughing Larch

Copyright © 2025 Creative Arts Management OÜ
All rights reserved.

Author: William Hawthorne
ISBN HARDBACK: 978-1-80567-181-7
ISBN PAPERBACK: 978-1-80567-480-1

## **Giggles Beneath the Boughs**

In the shade where shadows play,
Little creatures jump and sway.
Trees above wear silly hats,
Squirrels dance on gentle mats.

Laughter bubbles in the breeze,
Ticklish leaves that wobble with ease.
Branches twist in a playful tune,
As sunlight winks with a bright balloon.

**Dance of the Joyous Trees**

Branches sway with a cheeky flair,
Plotting pranks in the sweet spring air.
Roots tap-dance on the soft, warm ground,
Nature's laughter is all around.

Whispers echo through the green,
Breezy chuckles seldom seen.
Frogs join in with silly croaks,
While trees tell jokes, oh how they poke!

## Merriment on the Meadow

Flowers giggle, swaying bright,
Dancing shoes in morning light.
Butterflies with fluttering grins,
Join the waltz where joy begins.

Bees buzz softly, humming songs,
Nectar sippers, all day long.
Tickled petals, bright and bold,
With stories of the sun retold.

## **Serene Treetops in Spring**

In the heights where breezes tease,
Tall trees chuckle, bending knees.
With every gust, a hearty giggle,
Their laughter makes the sunlight wiggle.

Clouds drift by with playful sighs,
Painting smiles in the vast blue skies.
Joyful whispers spread like fire,
In the green, we find our choir.

## Silhouette of Smiles

In the trees where shadows sway,
Giggling leaves take flight and play.
Branches bow with joy, they sing,
Nature's jest, a merry fling.

Squirrels dance in silly loops,
With acorns flying, they're the troops.
Their chatter fills the warm, bright air,
A playful spirit everywhere.

Beneath the boughs, the sunlight beams,
Casting light on whimsical dreams.
Every rustle brings a grin,
In this space, we lose and win.

Laughter rings in every heart,
As fables flourish, nature's art.
In the woods, we chase the beat,
With every step, the world feels sweet.

## Sunny Interludes in the Pines

Dancing shadows on the ground,
Pine trees whisper, laughter's found.
Sunbeams tickle, spark the air,
Joyous giggles everywhere.

Mice in costumes, tails a-flare,
Play their parts without a care.
Silly songs on summer days,
Nature's jest in sunny rays.

Clouds above, they skip and twirl,
As breezes join the playful whirl.
A patch of mushrooms, hats on heads,
The forest floor in laughter spreads.

Underneath the azure dome,
Every critter feels at home.
In the pines, where mirth ignites,
The heart of nature, pure delights.

## The Whimsical Whisperer

In the clearing, dreams take flight,
With whispers soft, they light the night.
Grasshoppers play on drums of leaves,
In a forest dance, the spirit weaves.

Bouncing moss and breezy tunes,
Crickets join the night-time croons.
Moonlit paths, where shadows tease,
Beaming smiles upon the breeze.

A fox in jest, a prankster's game,
Leaves a trail of golden flame.
Hooting owls in wise disguise,
Laughing softly at our surprise.

Echoes of joy from tree to tree,
Nature whispers, wildly free.
In every rustle, laughter lingers,
The forest's fun, with painted fingers.

## Joyous Currents of the Forest

A river sparkles in delight,
Bubbles burst and dance in flight.
Fish that leap with glee and twirls,
Nature's laughter, pearls and swirls.

Jays that call in hoots of cheer,
Blossoms laugh as spring draws near.
With every flutter, every spin,
Joyful echoes reel us in.

Rabbits chase through grassy fields,
Snapping leaves, their mirth revealed.
A playful breeze, they leap and bound,
Where happiness and cheer abound.

In this haven, smiles collide,
Forever spreading, far and wide.
Through forest paths, we'll skip and glide,
With joyous currents as our guide.

## Beneath the Joyful Canopy

Underneath the leafy cheer,
Where giggles dance and swirl near.
The branches sway in playful jest,
Nature's smile, a welcomed guest.

Buds explode in vibrant hues,
As whispers tickle, chase the blues.
In this grove, the heart takes flight,
Laughter echoes through the night.

# Radiance of the Rustic

Brightly shines the woodland's face,
A tapestry of fun and grace.
Squirrels chatter, birds take wing,
In this place, the woods will sing.

Each twig and leaf, a jest to share,
With nature's charm beyond compare.
The sun peeks through with a wink,
And makes the flowers laugh and think.

**Laughter Within the Leaves**

A rustle from above takes flight,
Leaves giggle softly in delight.
As breezes play, they sway and tease,
Spreading joy upon the breeze.

The roots below hum a tune,
While critters dance beneath the moon.
A chorus rings from every bough,
Celebration fills here and now.

## Jubilant Puffs of Green

Fluffy clouds of emerald cheer,
Bouncing around without a fear.
Each twist and turn brings forth a grin,
In this riot, joy will win.

A jolly scene, where spirits race,
Nature's pranks fill every space.
With colors bright, the wild things play,
A carnival of green each day.

## Swaying Laughter in the Forest

In the glade where shadows play,
Branches dance and sway each day.
Leaves giggle, flutter, clash,
In a breezy, joyful bash.

Beneath the boughs, the creatures peek,
Squirrels wear a quirky cheek.
Owls chuckle, wise from high,
Watching as the breezes sigh.

Mushrooms smile in every hue,
Tickled by the morning dew.
Bouncing light like laughter spreads,
Whirling round where nature treads.

In this space of mirth and cheer,
Every plant and creature near.
Life's a jest, a playful lark,
Swaying joy within the park.

## Enchanted Laughter of the Trees

Amidst the trunks so broad and tall,
You hear the laughter rise, enthrall.
Chirping birds, a merry tune,
Underneath the shining moon.

Whimsical winds begin to tease,
Tickling leaves upon the breeze.
Twisting vines with giddy flair,
Dance in circles, light as air.

Roots together join the fun,
Telling tales of everyone.
With every rustle, laughter grows,
In the forest, joy bestows.

In this realm, let worries cease,
Join the chorus, find your peace.
For in the woods, all things align,
With playful giggles, summoning divine.

# Whispers in the Wind

Through whispering pines, a giggle flows,
Soft like secrets, no one knows.
Branches murmur, tales of cheer,
As the forest draws us near.

Frogs croak jokes by the stream,
Nature's humor, a lively dream.
Crickets chirp, their rhythm bold,
In hues of green and dappled gold.

The squirrels race from tree to tree,
Chasing laughter, wild and free.
Every rustling leaf and bloom,
Breathes delight, dispels the gloom.

In this space where wonders blend,
You'll find joy that has no end.
With every whistle, every cheer,
Life's a giggle, from ear to ear.

## Echoes of Euphoria

In the hollow where echoes ring,
Nature joins to hum and sing.
Trees do chuckle, roots entwined,
Sharing bliss with heart and mind.

Little critters, eyes aglow,
Scatter laughter on the flow.
Breezes carry joyful sound,
Riddles and rhymes that know no bound.

Foliage frolics, dances bright,
Under the playful sun's warm light.
Gently twirling, swaying leaves,
In this mirth, the spirit believes.

Join the fun, come take a peek,
In every corner, laughter's peak.
With echoes ringing through the air,
Feel euphoric, you're everywhere.

## Euphoria in the Evergreen

Beneath the trees where laughter grows,
A wiggly worm in silly clothes.
He dances round, a wobbly sight,
As squirrels giggle, day turns to night.

The branches sway, they twist and twirl,
While playful breezes make leaves whirl.
The pine cones drop with a comic thud,
Grasshoppers leap in a greenish flood.

Amid the pines, a jolly crew,
They sing of joy, not a single boo.
With every chuckle, the forest beams,
A kingdom built on wacky dreams.

So join the fun, take a hearty laugh,
In emerald halls, we'll dance and chap.
With every bark and cheeky grin,
Euphoria thrives where joy begins.

## **Whimsical Woods' Serenade**

In woodland realms where giggles sprout,
A raccoon prances with a vibrant shout.
He steals a snack from a squirrel's stash,
Then fumbles, tumbles, what a crash!

The shadows dance with spirits bold,
As trees share stories, both new and old.
A merry jig from the chipmunks' feet,
In a forest ballet, it's oh-so-sweet!

The ferns tremble with whispered cheer,
While owls chuckle, lending an ear.
The sun peeks through with a wink and a grin,
As merry melodies twirl in the din.

So lift your heart and join the spree,
Where whimsy winds through every tree.
With laughter's pulse, the woods do sway,
In this serenade, forever play.

## Gleeful Treasures of Nature

Among the trees, where giggles shine,
A clever fox spins tales divine.
He jests and teases, a playful rogue,
With every whim, he sparks the vogue.

The daisies chuckle, the sunflowers grin,
As butterflies frolic, letting fun begin.
Bees hum along to a jovial tune,
In a joyful dance 'neath the laughing moon.

The brook babbles with a cheeky jest,
While frogs leap high, they're put to the test.
With leaps and bounds, they join the play,
Each splash a smile, come what may.

So gather round for a nature spree,
Find treasures hidden in laughter's glee.
A kingdom bright with gleeful sights,
In nature's arms, the joy ignites.

## Joyful Shadows in the Thicket

In thickets deep where joy abounds,
A shadow dances, no sign of bounds.
A chubby bear with a wobbly walk,
Chimes in laughter, it's pure, not mock.

The branches creak with giggly spells,
A riddle spun from nature's wells.
A parade of critters, what a delight,
Each one eager to share their bite!

The rustling leaves play peek-a-boo,
As laughter echoes, the woods renew.
With whispers soft and pranks galore,
Joyful shadows come to explore.

So let us romp in this playful glen,
Where time is lost again and again.
Run with the shadows, let spirits soar,
In thicket dreams, we're forever more.

## Woodland Serenade

In the woods where shadows play,
A squirrel juggles nuts today.
Mice dance wearing tiny hats,
Chasing after playful cats.

The breeze whispers silly jokes,
While the wily fox just pokes.
Each plant sways with delight,
Underneath the soft moonlight.

Trees shake their branches tall,
As if preparing for a ball.
Frogs croak in a cheerful tune,
Crafting rhythms 'neath the moon.

Laughter echoes through the glade,
While the chipmunks laugh and parade.
Nature's humor, oh so bright,
Indulges all—what a sight!

## Jolly Statement of the Seasons

Spring arrives with a playful wink,
Flowers giggle, making us think.
Birds chirp with an upbeat song,
All of nature hums along.

Summer's here—a clownish sun,
Bright balloons and endless fun.
The bees buzz in a silly dance,
Each petal sways in a trance.

Autumn's jesters, leaves unwind,
Crunchy laughter fills the mind.
Pumpkins grin in fields aglow,
Telling tales from long ago.

Winter brings its frosty cheer,
Snowflakes twirl, they spin and steer.
Snowmen joke with carrot noses,
In a land where laughter dozes.

**Grins among the Forest Giants**

Beneath the giants tall and grand,
A playful rabbit sparks a band.
Frogs leap in a giddy craze,
While pebbles dance in summer's haze.

The wise old oak begins to sway,
Telling tales of yesterday.
A caterpillar hums with zest,
It knows how to be the best.

Crickets chirp their nightly song,
With rhythm smooth and oh so strong.
Stars twinkle like they've made a pact,
To grace the stage, the forest act.

Glorious giggles pierce the night,
As creatures twirl in pure delight.
Nature chuckles, full of glee,
In this realm, they laugh in spree.

## Lightheartedness in the Leafage

Leaves flutter down in twists and spins,
As playful air around them grins.
Chirpy whips of breezy fun,
Through every branch, they swiftly run.

A butterfly dons a costume bright,
Dancing joy in morning light.
The mushrooms sport their dots of cheer,
Welcoming all who wander near.

Rabbits play hide-and-seek in rows,
While the wise old turtle knows how it goes.
With every rustle, sounds of glee,
Spark laughter in the woodsy spree.

Beneath the canopy's playful veil,
Joy dances in each story's trail.
In the rustling leaves, a chorus born,
Nature's laughs, forever worn.

**Sprightly Songs of the Wilderness**

In the forest, voices rise,
Squirrels chatter, birds surprise.
Branches dance in playful sway,
Whispers echo, laugh away.

Mushrooms giggle on the ground,
Nature's jokes, a joy profound.
Wind tickles leaves with gentle cheer,
Tree trunks chuckle, loud and clear.

## Heartbeats of Happiness

A fox trots with a jaunty stride,
Winks at others, full of pride.
Breezes carry bursts of glee,
As critters paint their jubilee.

Bubbles form in puddles small,
Frogs jump in for a splishy-fall.
Laughter rings through every glade,
Joyful moments never fade.

## **Giggling Greenery**

Among the ferns where shadows play,
Laughter blooms in bright array.
Dappled sunlight flickers bright,
Nature's joke is pure delight.

Breezes rustle, secrets shared,
Witty plants that have all dared.
Every leaf a smile so wide,
In this land, pure joy resides.

## Elation in the Evergreen

Evergreens stand tall and proud,
Swaying gently, laughter loud.
Dancing shadows, twinkling light,
Whimsy weaves through day and night.

Critters gather, form a crew,
Singing songs both bright and blue.
Joy spills over, fills the air,
In this realm, all hearts declare.

## Euphoria Among the Elms

In a grove where giggles bloom,
Trees sway like dancers in a room.
Branches whisper playful tunes,
Tickling all beneath the moons.

Leaves chuckle, rustling bright,
Bouncing beams of sheer delight.
Squirrels wear their hats askew,
Jumping high in lively view.

Bees buzz with a comical sting,
Chasing shadows as they swing.
Even the moss grins on the ground,
Joyful echoes all around.

In this patch of silly cheer,
Every face is full of cheer.
Nature's jesters, light and free,
Bring euphoria endlessly.

## Smiles in Sunlit Spaces

Underneath the broad sun's rays,
Nature jests in playful ways.
Breezes nudge the branches wide,
Inviting all to join the ride.

Dandelions toss their heads,
Chasing laughter in their beds.
A rabbit sports a jaunty cap,
Leaping joy with every clap.

Glimmers dance on petals' seam,
Weaving tales from dream to dream.
In this theatre of delight,
Laughter finds its shining light.

Whether it's the roots or leaves,
Every element believes,
Life's a jest, a happy race,
Spreading smiles in sunlit space.

## Woodland Whirlwind

In a forest thick with cheer,
Nature spins the tales we hear.
Twisting vines in funny shapes,
Make way for the giggling apes.

The squirrels prance on branches high,
While butterflies twirl in the sky.
Acorns roll with humor sweet,
Beneath the dancers' nimble feet.

Every rustle brings a laugh,
Echoes of a woodland staff.
Whirlwinds swirl in playful glee,
A merry match of wild spree.

Beneath the boughs, we can see,
Joy unfolds like fun spree.
In this dance of leaf and breeze,
Laughter flows with perfect ease.

## Revelry of the Resplendent

With colors bright and sounds so clear,
The woods ring out a song sincere.
Every critter, big and small,
Joins the revelry, one and all.

Chirping birds with winking eyes,
Conceive a plot of bright surprise.
A fox in jest, a bear that prances,
Nature's ball in silly dances.

Sunlight dapples through the leaves,
Laughter grows as nature weaves.
Underneath this vibrant dome,
Every creature feels at home.

So run and play, don't mind the hours,
In this realm of blooming flowers.
Reveling in a joyful spree,
The resplendence sets us free.

## A Symphony of Smiles

In a grove where chuckles bloom,
Leaves dance with a gentle tune,
Branches sway, a playful flare,
Nature's jesters, light as air.

Squirrels tease on a playful run,
Chasing shadows, having fun,
Whispers of laughter fill the breeze,
Tickling branches with such ease.

Beneath the sun, a joyful sight,
Colors spark, pure delight,
Roots of humor stretch and twist,
A merry buzz, we can't resist.

In this park, we shed our frowns,
Giggling trees in leafy crowns,
With every rustle, giggles soar,
A symphony we all adore.

## Glee Amid the Giants

Amidst the giants standing tall,
Laughter echoes, a cheerful call,
Leaves burst forth with a vibrant grin,
Ticklish tendrils beckon us in.

A wise old trunk tells jokes so sly,
As sunlight plays, we can't deny,
Bouncing boughs sway with delight,
Amid the green, we take flight.

Roots that wiggle under our feet,
Dance and jive, a rhythm sweet,
Nature's silly, whimsical dance,
Invites us all to take a chance.

Under the broad, embracing shade,
Joyful moments, never fade,
With every whisper, they declare,
Glee is woven everywhere.

## Trees that Tickle the Heart

In a sunny glen where laughter grows,
Trees share tales that everyone knows,
Giggles echo through the leaves,
As nature plays and mischief weaves.

Every branch a crooked smile,
Inviting us to stay a while,
Bark that chuckles, roots that play,
Whimsical charms light up the day.

Laughter ripples through the air,
Joyful moments without a care,
Like playful sprites in a friendly game,
These gentle giants, never the same.

When shadows stretch and evening falls,
Their whispers dance along the walls,
A hidden joy, a secret part,
These trees just tickle the heart.

**Pondering Brightness**

In every leaf, a thought resides,
Giggling softly as the sun slides,
Branches pondering, shadows play,
Brightness spoken in a playful way.

With every breeze, a chuckle spreads,
Waking dreams from cozy beds,
Nature's muse with a gleeful twist,
Sings to us in a joy-filled mist.

Whimsy twirls around the trunks,
In this realm where laughter clunks,
Every step, a joyful dance,
Inviting all to join the chance.

Around the bend where echoes cling,
A gentle heart, a song to sing,
Brightness lingers, sweet and smart,
Pondering joy, a work of art.

**Whispers of Joyful Pines**

In the forest where laughter sways,
Pines chuckle in their own funny ways.
Branches sway with a playful shout,
Tickling the winds that dance about.

Squirrels pause, with cheeky grins,
Sharing secrets, where joy begins.
Each rustle, a giggle so bright,
Echoing softly into the night.

## Echoes in the Woodland Breeze

Breezes carry whispers of glee,
Amongst the trees, so wild and free.
Leaves flutter, their laughter spread,
A symphony of joy overhead.

With each swirl, a tickle in the air,
Branches wave as if they care.
Nature's humor in every sound,
In this playful world, joy is found.

**Grinning Boughs Under Moonlight**

Moonlight casts a goofy glow,
On branches that sway to and fro.
Laughter rings through the night,
As creatures join in delight.

A rabbit hops with a bounce so spry,
Underneath the starry sky.
Grinning boughs share a playful jest,
The forest feels like a lively fest.

## Treetops' Delighted Revelry

In the canopy, a party in sway,
Where treetops laugh, come join the play.
Every rustle, a joyous cheer,
Nature's glee is ever near.

With each gust, the laughter flows,
As woodland creatures strike poses.
Branches bow in a merry spree,
Creating a jest for all to see.

# Giggles in the Canopy

Beneath the branches, whispers play,
A tickle of breeze, brightens the day.
Squirrels chatter, in jolly delight,
They dive and they dart, a comical sight.

Sunbeams dance in an amber swirl,
Where feathered jesters spin and twirl.
A branch bows low, it nearly broke,
As leaves erupt in a hearty joke.

The shadows wiggle, a playful tease,
And laughter echoes on the breeze.
Little creatures in silly parade,
Turn the forest into a grand charade.

Among the trunks, giggles resound,
As nature's jesters frolic around.
Join in the fun, step into the sun,
In this leafy realm, we all can run.

## Serene Sylvan Chuckles

In the heart of the woods, giggles arise,
With branches that bounce beneath wide blue skies.
Every rustle is wrapped in a grin,
As laughter and joy weave their way in.

Fluffy clouds form a whimsical show,
While gentle breezes whisper below.
A ticklish leaf lands right on your nose,
And warmth wraps around, as mischief grows.

The forest floor, a patchwork of play,
Where silly antics brighten the day.
A band of owls with winked eyes stare,
And frolicsome critters leap everywhere.

As happiness blooms on each branch and side,
The woodlands burst forth in riotous pride.
Dance with the shadows, embrace the spree,
In this cheerful spot, come laugh with me.

## Pine Cone Jests in Autumn

In autumn's embrace, with colors ablaze,
Pine cones tumble down in a merry daze.
They roll and they bounce, a playful parade,
Painting the ground in a nutty charade.

The critters gather with squeaks of delight,
As acorns and leaves join the frolicsome fight.
The branches, they giggle at the raucous fun,
While golden rays dance with the setting sun.

A punchy breeze sends giggles through trees,
As rustling leaves-laugh at their own tease.
With a bounce and a roll, the jokes never end,
In this riot of autumn, all hearts will mend.

So join in the frolic, let spirits ignite,
For humor and joy make the forest's delight.
With each tumble and fall, let laughter be found,
In this merry realm of nature unbound.

## Merriment Amongst the Needles

Amongst the needles, the giggles do soar,
Where each bristle and bough holds stories galore.
Pine trees chuckle in the soft evening glow,
Creating a stage where the silly winds blow.

Little birds flit with a vibrant display,
Singing sweet tunes in a riotous way.
A gentle breeze carries whispers of cheer,
As laughter and joy fill the atmosphere.

From acorns to saplings, the pranks unfold,
Nature reveals all her wonders untold.
Twisting and turning with each trickster's game,
Every giggle and snicker is never the same.

So stroll through the needles, with joy in your heart,
Let merriment blossom, let laughter take part.
In the forest where whimsy and joy intertwine,
Embrace every chuckle, for here it's divine.

## Laughing Leaves of Autumn

Gold and crimson dance in the breeze,
Whirling together, they giggle with ease.
A rustle of jokes in the cool, crisp air,
Nature's chuckles, a light-hearted affair.

Squirrels scamper with acorn delight,
Their tails twitching, a comical sight.
Around every tree, laughter does bloom,
As whispers of humor chase away gloom.

From branches above, a chorus rings clear,
Leaves howl with laughter, drawing us near.
Each fluttering flap a mischievous tease,
The sun shines down, warming the peas.

In the crispness found in this autumn's cheer,
Laughter resounds for all hearts to hear.
So dance with the leaves, let your spirit fly,
For nature's jesters can never say goodbye.

## Nature's Ticklish Touch

Breezes whisper secrets, a playful parade,
Sunlight tickles, in shadows it wade.
The brook bubbles over with giggles and glee,
Nature plays pranks, oh, so merrily!

Mischievous bees buzz round, singing their tunes,
Wagging their wings like jolly balloons.
Flowers burst open with fits of sweet laughter,
Echoes of joy, a blissful disaster.

Clouds roll in laughter, they tumble and swell,
Painting the skies where the sunlight fell.
Each drop of rain joins in on the fun,
Splashes of humor when daytime is done.

In this vibrant playground where whimsy won't quit,
Nature's touch tickles with each little bit.
So dance through the meadows, let giggles abound,
For joy is the treasure in life's playful sound.

# Enchanted Laughs Beneath the Sky

Underneath the arch of the wide open blue,
Nature tells stories where the wild wind blew.
With each little whisper, a chuckle is found,
As creatures unite, with joy all around.

The playful pixies weave their bright spells,
With sparkles of laughter, they beckon and swell.
A daisy leans in to hear what they say,
Sharing a giggle, they brighten the day.

In the soft, golden light, shadows waltz true,
The pine trees lean close, joining the view.
They cackle with tickles, bark out a cheer,
A symphony of fun for all who draw near.

So let your heart echo the giggles so free,
In this magical realm, lose the burden and see.
With each splashing moment, let laughter arise,
A tapestry woven 'neath infinite skies.

## Forest of Fanciful Whispers

In the heart of the woods where the tall trees sway,
Fanciful whispers make spirits play.
With every rustle, secrets are shared,
Laughter dances freely, completely unprepared.

The mushrooms wear hats like they're ready to party,
While critters exchange tales at the top of the stardy.
Each flicker of light brings joy to the night,
Under starlit eyes, pure laughter takes flight.

Bouncing along paths where shadows engage,
The forest is bursting with joy on each page.
Cicadas join in with their jubilant song,
Creating a choir that feels ever so strong.

So wander through chirps and chuckles galore,
In this whimsical place, there's always more.
Let the fanciful whispers enchant every ear,
For in the forest's heart, joy is ever near.

## Woodland Wizards of Wit

In the woods where quirks arise,
Frogs don hats and start to rise.
Squirrels dance with nutty flair,
While shadows giggle in mid-air.

Among the trees where laughter swells,
A raccoon spins with silly bells.
Mice in cloaks begin to prance,
Every rustle leads to a dance.

With whispers carrying on the breeze,
Ye olde owl joins with a tease.
The mossy floor, a stage so bright,
Where every critter shares delight.

So join the jest of woodland glee,
Where laughter's woven in the trees.
Each giggle is a sweet refrain,
In this realm where joy's the gain.

## Dance of the Gilded Branches

Up above where the sunlight plays,
Branches twirl in golden rays.
A squirrel jigs with tails held high,
While feathers flutter from the sky.

The branches shimmy, shining bright,
As sunbeams spark in sheer delight.
The forest floor joins the cheer,
Echoes of laughter fill the sphere.

Woodpeckers drum a silly beat,
While merry frogs hop on their feet.
Each leaf whispers secrets of fun,
Beneath the shimmering midday sun.

With every twist, the forest beams,
In this dance, we share our dreams.
Laughter mingles with the breeze,
A joyful bond among the trees.

## Smiles Amidst the Forest Floor

Amidst the ferns, a chuckle grows,
As daisies dance and the breezy blows.
Beneath the shade, a picnic lay,
Where critters dine and jest all day.

Ants march on with tiny pies,
While butterflies float in the skies.
A hedgehog jokes in prickly style,
Making everyone pause and smile.

Breezes carry whispers of cheer,
In this woodland, laughter draws near.
The flower beds bloom in delight,
As the sun bids farewell to night.

Underneath the smiling trees,
Nature's magic unfolds with ease.
With every giggle, joy restores,
Together we love our forest floors.

## Cheerful Cones and Chirps

Pinecones giggle, tossed about,
While little birds join in the shout.
Their chirps collide in playful spree,
A symphony of habitat glee.

Underneath the towering pines,
Whimsical creatures draw bright lines.
Laughter bounces in every nook,
Their joy is found in every look.

From branches high to roots below,
The woodland raves with a vibrant glow.
Every shadow hides a grin,
Inviting us to laugh within.

So let us dance through fields of green,
Among the trees where joy is seen.
With cheerful cones and chirps so bright,
We'll weave our dreams in pure delight.

## Echoes of Woodland Whimsy

In the glen where giggles sprout,
Trees sway with a joyful shout,
Squirrels jest in merry tune,
Beneath the watchful crescent moon.

Mushrooms dance in polka spots,
Ants parade in funny thoughts,
Every critter, every sprite,
Shares a laugh in pure delight.

The brook chuckles, water sings,
Tickling roots of ancient things,
Frogs croon their silly croaks,
Nature's stage for timeless jokes.

Hidden nooks and peeking eyes,
Whispers float like wind-blown sighs,
Magic lingers, laughter swells,
In this place where joy compels.

## **Jocular Shadows at Dusk**

As evening casts its playful veil,
Shadows giggle, tell a tale,
Bouncing beams of fading light,
Wobble like a feathered kite.

Crickets play a syncopated beat,
While fireflies skip on nimble feet,
Every rustle rings with glee,
Whispering secrets to the trees.

A squirrel dons a tiny hat,
While rabbits roll and tumble flat,
The moon chuckles, dim and bright,
In the frolic of the night.

Each root and bough, a merry jest,
Partying in nature's fest,
Together in this twilight scheme,
Echoing a woodland dream.

## Sprightly Twirls of Leafy Laughter

In a canopy of swaying fun,
Leaves twist, twirl, laugh, and run,
Breezes carry whispers light,
Tickling branches, oh such delight!

Hopping hares with antics bright,
Chase the shadows into the night,
Dancing daisies join the play,
In this meadow's grand display.

A wise old owl with twinkling eyes,
Snores aloud, the humor flies,
With every hoot, a chuckle spreads,
Filling the woods with joy instead.

The grass quivers, bursting free,
With jokes only nature can see,
In every rustle, every breeze,
The laughter of the forest trees.

## Frolic of the Forest Spirits

Wimbling whispers wind through trees,
Where spirits frolic with such ease,
Twirling in a vibrant dance,
Nature's laugh, a wild romance.

Pixies prance on cushions soft,
While mushrooms giggle, lift aloft,
Sunbeams tickle, tugging light,
Squirrels wobble in pure delight.

The evening hue in hues so bright,
Echoes of joy, with pure delight,
A hidden wink behind the bark,
Laughter lingers in the dark.

In every flutter, every grace,
The silly sprites find their place,
Each chuckle ripples, sweet and clear,
In the forest, joy is near.

## The Enchanted Grove of Merriment

In a grove of giggles, trees do sway,
With branches dancing, come what may.
Leaves whisper jokes in breezy tones,
While critters chuckle, skipping stones.

Beneath the sun, a squirrel pranced,
Wore a tiny hat and sweetly danced.
The mushrooms grinned, all round and bright,
In this fun-filled realm, pure delight.

Nearby a brook, the frogs regale,
Croaking sonnets, hearty and hale.
A rabbit winks, with mischief rife,
In this merry place, joy springs to life.

So come and play, let laughter ring,
In the enchanted grove, where hearts can sing.

## Boughs of Bliss

Under boughs of bliss, the antics unfold,
With playful shadows, stories are told.
Squirrels in capes, heroes of the day,
Swinging and twirling, they lead the way.

The flowers chuckle, petals a-flutter,
Dancing in rhythm, not a moment to utter.
While butterflies chase their giggling friends,
In this joyful grove, the laughter never ends.

A wise old owl, perched high on a limb,
Shares puns and giggles, while others join in.
In the golden light, fun-loving and spry,
Joyful echoes linger, beneath the bright sky.

## Carousel of Colors and Chuckles

Spin through colors, bright and bold,
On this carousel, laughter is gold.
The trees swirl around, in a merry spree,
Painting the air with giggles, you see!

Leaves take flight, like confetti tossed,
In this wonderland, no joy is lost.
Daisies wear crowns, the roses sing loud,
Each bloom a jester, under the shroud.

A parade of critters joins in the fun,
With wobbly steps, they dance in the sun.
The melody of mirth, a sweet serenade,
In this magical realm, pure joy is made.

## Forest Frolics

In the heart of the woods, where laughter thrives,
Creatures abound, in their joyous dives.
Frogs in tuxedos croon a tune,
While squirrels applaud, beneath the moon.

Dancing with shadows, the trees sway along,
In playful harmony, a whimsical song.
The flowers giggle, swaying in breeze,
Tickling the fancy of buzzing bees.

The night brings tales of frolicsome glee,
With whispers of mischief, from each leafy tree.
Through the winding paths, let your spirit roam,
In this forest of fun, you're never alone.

## Laughter Beneath the Bark

In a grove where giggles dwell,
Branches sway, and secrets tell.
Squirrels dance, a merry sight,
Tickling leaves in pure delight.

The sunbeam's playful rays will tease,
With shadows prancing on the breeze.
Nature's chuckles, soft and bright,
Whisper life in morning light.

A swing of vines, an acorn's roll,
The woodland's jest, a merry toll.
Mossy cushions, laughter's seat,
Every step, a joyful beat.

Amidst the pines, a hearty cheer,
Echoes of joy, they soar and clear.
In every rustle, nature's jest,
A jubilant heart, forever blessed.

## Forest's Playful Heart

Where sunlight beams through leafy crowns,
The forest wears its jester's gowns.
Mischievous winds swirl and swoon,
Dancing leaves like bright balloons.

A rabbit hops with cheeky flair,
Nose twitching without a care.
In every nook, a tale unfolds,
Whispered giggles, laughter bold.

Frogs croak jokes while crickets sing,
Silly songs the owls can bring.
Nature's spirit, wild and free,
Rings with jokes from every tree.

As shadows stretch and daylight wanes,
The woodland plays, it never feigns.
Under the stars, a playful art,
The glowing night, the forest's heart.

## Bursting with Nature's Glee

Among the boughs, a chuckle flows,
Where every breeze, a story knows.
Wildflowers grin in colors bright,
Painting fields with pure delight.

The brook babbles a funny tale,
As raindrops dance with sprightly ale.
In this wild realm where smiles convene,
Joy springs forth, a lively scene.

Frolicking foxes, playful and spry,
Chasing dreams 'neath an azure sky.
With every leap, a heart takes flight,
Bursting forth with pure delight.

Among the trees, a raucous cheer,
Nature's whimsy ringing clear.
Life's a jest, as day turns free,
In this realm of harmony.

# Chortling Hollow of Green

In chortling woods, where laughter reigns,
Every tree a trickster, no one complains.
Birds crack jokes on branches high,
With the breeze as their silly ally.

Beneath the ferns, a party's begun,
Where critters, cocktail drinks are spun.
Whispers bright as sunshine's gleam,
Tickle the roots where dreams teem.

A wiggly worm with sense of style,
Waves to the crowd with a cheeky smile.
In this hollow, joy does bloom,
Filling the air with a bright perfume.

As twilight falls and shadows tease,
Laughter echoes through lush leaves.
In every stump, a joyous scene,
A playful heart, forever green.

## Cheering Canopy of Green

In the shade where shadows play,
Trees whisper in a breezy sway,
Squirrels dance with a cheeky grin,
Branches sway, let the fun begin!

Leaves chuckle with every breeze,
Nature's jester, swaying trees,
Beneath the boughs, laughter's song,
Time slips by; it won't be long!

Sunlight filters, a playful gleam,
Sunshine smiles, a vibrant beam,
Every critter joins the fun,
In this green, we leap and run!

Faces bright with joy abound,
In this haven, mirth is found,
Eager hearts and spirits free,
Join the dance, just you and me!

## Joy Beneath the Branches

Underneath the playful leaves,
Giggles dance where nature weaves,
Twigs and vines in merry swirl,
A symphony of life unfurl.

Chirpy birds join in the jest,
Each little note, a happy quest,
Rustling charm of laughter's cheer,
In this nook, we've naught to fear!

Dancing shadows on soft ground,
Bouncing joy is all around,
Within the greens, we spin and sway,
A magical and funny day!

Beneath the boughs, we sing and play,
Nature's stage in grand display,
In the leaves, the breezes tease,
Delightful chuckles on the breeze!

## Whimsy among the Woodlands

A caper here, a frolic there,
Nature's laughter fills the air,
Whimsical paths where we roam,
In this green, we find our home.

Jigs and jumps, the critters prance,
In the sunlight, they do dance,
Every leaf, a giggling muse,
Sharing smiles, we cannot lose!

Frogs croak jokes from lily leaves,
While buzzing bees weave in and weave,
With playful wind, we toss our cares,
In this place, delight compares!

Chasing shadows, we won't stop,
Round and round, we laugh and hop,
Joy abounds in every glance,
Step in rhythm, join the dance!

## Spirit of the Sunlit Grove

In the glade where sunlight beams,
Laughter flows like bubbling streams,
Leaves congregate in joyful play,
Whispering secrets, come what may.

Branches stretch with cheerful grace,
Nature wears a friendly face,
In the bright, we spin and twirl,
A world of wonder, watch it swirl!

Frolicking in hues so bright,
Every shadow brings delight,
Running wild, we're full of cheer,
In the grove, we have no fear!

Mirthful echoes through the trees,
Happiness rides on the breeze,
Join in laughter, feel the glow,
In this haven, let it flow!

## The Humorous Timberland

In a grove where the jokes grow wide,
Trees chuckle with every swing and slide.
Branches dance to a whimsical tune,
Squirrels giggle beneath the moon.

Droplets of rain drop like laughter,
Splashing in puddles, chasing after.
Mushrooms wear hats of vivid hues,
While the sunbeams play peek-a-boo.

The fox tells tales that twist and turn,
As ferns listen with hearts ablaze and burn.
Breezes whistle in cheeky delight,
Kicking up leaves in a playful flight.

So join the revels, don't delay,
In this woodland wonderland of play.
Each trunk a confidant, every vine a joke,
Amongst the trees, let laughter provoke!

## Joy's Winding Path

On a trail where giggles greet the day,
Bouncing blooms join in on the play.
With every step, the ground hums cheer,
A jocular journey to bring all near.

A clumsy rabbit hops into a bush,
Sending squirrels into a wild rush.
Hiccups from hedgehogs, or so it seems,
Echo laughter woven in dreams.

Nuts roll down paths in a merry chase,
Wonky acorns spin in a dance of grace.
The wind tosses whispers, teasing the air,
While echoes of chuckles bounce everywhere.

Follow the trail, don't hesitate,
A whimsical world in which we create.
Every turn a surprise, every bend a laugh,
Winding through joy, a fanciful path!

## **Hilarity at the Forest's Edge**


Where the trees swap stories in vibrant tones,
Laughter rings where the wild critters roam.
Banshee owls with tales of old,
Recounting mischief that never gets old.

The brook speaks in splashes, a giggling glee,
Playing pranks on the roots of the tree.
Toads sing ballads in ribbits and croaks,
Choruses of whimsy from hardened folks.

Wind chimes jingle with a playful sound,
Tickling branches that sway all around.
Underfoot, furry creatures caper,
With antics that could rival any paper.

Edge of the woods, where the fun ignites,
Join the ruckus, delight in the sights.
With humor abound and smiles in range,
A laugh from the wild, forever strange!

## Crescendo of Cheer

In the heart of the woods, merriment swells,
As woodpeckers drum on their rhythmic bells.
Creeping vines whisper ridiculous tales,
While rabbits crack jokes as the sun prevails.

With each fluttering leaf, laughter collects,
Responses that bounce, what a place to reflect!
A chorus of chuckles, both soft and loud,
Echoing joy in a forest so proud.

The compass of humor points everywhere,
Leading us onward without any care.
Sunflowers beam, with faces so bright,
Tickled by breezes that dance in the light.

Crescendo of laughter, oh what a treat,
In every corner, surprises repeat.
Join in the rapture, let happiness flow,
In this cheerful grove, let good spirits grow!

## The Merry Mirage

In a field where shadows dance,
Whispers jest, a cheerful prance.
Tickling winds, a playful breeze,
Leaves chuckle, swaying with ease.

Branches twist like silly grins,
Nature's laughter softly spins.
Among the blooms, a jesters' choir,
Tickled pink with sun's desire.

Glossy beetles race with flair,
Bumblebees swing without a care.
Mirth spills forth, no frown in sight,
Daylight shimmers, pure delight.

Petals giggle, colors bright,
Dancing under soft moonlight.
Magic plays in every sway,
Join the jest, come out and play!

## Harmony of the Wilderness

In a realm where the wild things sing,
Every creature wears a silly wing.
Squirrels caper, acorns in hand,
Nature's jest in a merry band.

Frogs croak jokes in a ribbit show,
While fireflies twinkle, putting on glow.
Trees roll their eyes as owls take flight,
Under moon's gaze, all feels just right.

In the brook, fish twirl and glide,
With a splash, they join the ride.
Laughter bubbles, a sweet refrain,
As night whispers secrets again.

A tapestry of chuckles sewn,
Joy in every heart that's grown.
Join the wild in laughter's embrace,
In harmony, we find our place!

## Garlands of Glee

Upon the hill, a feast of cheer,
Sprightly flowers bend to hear.
With petals bright and colors loud,
They gather 'round, a jolly crowd.

Bouncing bees with stripes of gold,
Tell of stories, funny and bold.
Daisies giggle, standing tall,
Joined by laughter, sprouting all.

Butterflies dance, twirling on air,
With every flap, they banish care.
A waltz ensues in vibrant hues,
In this garden, nothing to lose.

Mirthful vines twist and twine,
Creating garlands, so divine.
In every nook, giggles conceal,
Life's sweet joy, a perfect reel!

## Gladsome Forest Frolic

Beneath the boughs, a lively spree,
Dance of leaves in jubilee.
Rustling laughter fills the air,
As squirrels play without a care.

Mice in pockets, toadstools cheer,
Spin their tales for all to hear.
With every rustle, the branches glee,
Nature's stage, a grand marquee.

Woodland creatures in party hats,
Joining in with energetic chats.
Hopping rabbits, ever so spry,
Bounce along, reach for the sky.

At dusk the fireflies start their dance,
Swaying 'neath the stars, a trance.
In laughter's light, we take delight,
Together forever, our hearts ignite!

## Joyful Shadows at Dusk

In twilight's glow, shadows prance,
The trees waltz in a silly dance.
Leaves flutter down, like giggles in air,
While whispers of wind play without a care.

A squirrel slips, a chirp takes flight,
As nature chuckles at day turning night.
Beneath the boughs, we share the glee,
In playful moments, wild and free.

A branch bows low, a swing for fun,
Where sunlight dips, the day is done.
Laughter lingers, in paths we tread,
A merry chorus, where joy is spread.

With every rustle, a joke does bloom,
As crickets chirp a tune to whom?
Around the roots, the spirits roam,
In evening's blush, we find our home.

## Nature's Playful Ballad

Amidst the trees, where laughter sings,
A patchwork quilt of joyful things.
The brook babbles jokes as it flows,
Sprightly banter, nobody knows.

Beneath the boughs, a rabbit slides,
In a waddle that no one hides.
A butterfly flutters with a wink,
While secrets are spilled in a drink.

The grass wears crowns of daisy lace,
As sunshine spills into each face.
With every breeze, a playful sigh,
And giggles linger as clouds pass by.

Nature's jesters juggle and hop,
In a whirlwind of chuckles that never stop.
Join the revel, come dance along,
In this merry world where you belong.

## Radiance in the Green Canopy

A shimmer bright between the leaves,
Where every twinkling spirit weaves.
The branches sway with whimsy's cheer,
As sunlight tickles, laughing near.

A fox rolls over, a playful act,
While shadows echo the funny fact.
With every rustle, a giggle spreads,
As nature's tapestry keeps us fed.

Petals dance with a breezy tease,
While buzzing bees hum songs with ease.
The sunbeams sparkle on dewy grass,
Like laughter shared in a merry mass.

From tree to tree, the jokes do fly,
As every critter skips on by.
In this canopy where joy prevails,
The laughter lingers, and love never fails.

## **Gales of Delight**

When gales of joy swirl high and free,
A dandelion makes a wish with glee.
The clouds chase each other in playful flight,
As gentle breezes share delight.

A chipmunk scurries, a pinch of sass,
Through fields of laughter, it wiggles past.
Each rustle and tickle ignites the air,
With nature's giggles bursting everywhere.

The sun dips low, a glowing smile,
Inviting all to linger a while.
With every branch that twists and bends,
The world is wrapped in joyful trends.

So come and dance in gales of light,
Join in the laughter, feel the delight.
For in this realm where the silly play,
Every moment shines, come join the fray.

## The Jocular Roots

In the grove where shadows play,
The trees spin tales both night and day.
A squirrel dons a jester's cap,
And giggles wrap the world in a clap.

Ticklish twigs sway with a cheer,
Whispers of humor drawn near.
Beneath the canopy, laughter takes flight,
As breezes chuckle in the fading light.

Bark-wrapped friends share jokes from above,
Plenty of folly and trees full of love.
The forest floor dances, a comical spree,
Where nature's laughter is wild and free.

Through swaying branches, the jokes take root,
And shoes filled with mud don't follow suit.
The jovial chorus from every beat,
Keeps the woodland alive on its feet.

## Laughing Aliases of Nature

A breeze blew by with a tickle and grin,
Nature's chuckles beneath the skin.
Every petal bursts in splendid jest,
As flora trades puns, none is the best.

The river gurgles with a witty stream,
Tickling rocks as it weaves its dream.
Laughter echoes in the babbling song,
Each ripple a giggle all day long.

Mischievous clouds in the sky's blue vault,
Dodge the sun like a graceful waltz.
With a punchline hidden in every shade,
The horizons are brightened, fears allayed.

Nature wears joy as a vibrant cloak,
Here, every bark and leaf can joke.
With every rustle, a funny twist,
No solemn face can dare exist.

## Lively Lattes of Larch

In a café of trees where the branches brew,
Mugfuls of laughter seep through the dew.
Cup after cup, the humor pours wide,
Tickling the roots that dance and glide.

Frothy fronds swirl in a playful tease,
As sunlight quips on a gentle breeze.
The acorns giggle, a comedy show,
While sap runs up with a punchline flow.

Each sip brings whispers of playful cheer,
As whimsical critters all gather near.
With mugs made of leaves, they share a warm chat,
No worries allowed, only joy where they sat.

And when the twilight wraps all in its lace,
The forest shares smiles, a jovial embrace.
So join the banquet where roots tune the string,
And find in each sip, the joy that they bring.

## Smiling Soliloquy in the Glade

In a glade where the sunlight winks bright,
Grass blades crack jokes, with sheer delight.
A curious fox prances, tips its hat,
To the twirling leaves, what's up with that?

A scene unfolds with a giggle and squeal,
Nature's oddities make it surreal.
Flowers dance round in a joyful parade,
Where every petal's a prankster, unafraid.

In this concert of laughter, each creature plays,
With whimsy and joy wrapping their days.
The pond reflects surprised faces so bold,
In ripples of joy, their stories unfold.

As night falls soft with stars all aglow,
The whispers of mirth in the shadows still flow.
In this theater of joy, no frown can invade,
For even the moon finds a punchline that stayed.

## Mirth Amidst the Saplings

In the woods where shadows play,
Tiny trees dance in their sway.
Squirrels chuckle on their way,
Branches jiggle, bright as day.

Frogs in jest leap with delight,
Clouds above drift, pure and white.
Breezy whispers, soft and light,
Nature's laughter feels just right.

## Nature's Hilarious Harmony

Amidst the leaves, a buzz and cheer,
A rabbit hops, it draws near.
Singing birds lend a warm ear,
Jokes exchanged in laughter clear.

Buzzing bees with tunes to share,
Petals twirl without a care.
Joyful echoes fill the air,
Nature's jest is everywhere.

## **Jolly Luminescence of Foliage**

Golden rays through green leaves peek,
Wisps of sunlight play and sneak.
Fungi chuckle, colors unique,
Laughter blooms, oh so mystique!

Dancing shadows, a motley crew,
Giggling breezes swirl and skew.
Every branch, a knotted view,
Where humor thrives beneath the blue.

## Cheery Echoes of the Grove

Under canopies, the chuckles rise,
Woodpeckers knock in sweet surprise.
In the thickets, joy complies,
Nature's fun beneath wide skies.

Whimsical creatures take their chance,
In the foliage, all join the dance.
Life is sweet, a fleeting trance,
Rhythms blend in merry prance.

## The Tree that Tells Jokes

In the woods where whispers play,
A tree stands tall, brightening the day.
With branches swaying, it starts to share,
Jokes that flutter through the air.

The squirrels stop, their cheeks so full,
As they giggle, they dance and pull.
Each punchline brings a burst of cheer,
Echoing laughter that all can hear.

Birds join in, chirping with glee,
Branches bounce, it's quite the spree!
The forest chuckles, trees in sync,
A merry sight, with smiles to link.

So if you wander down this way,
Listen close, come laugh and stay.
For in this grove of humor's grace,
Joyful giggles fill the space.

## Sprightly Sway of the Needles

Sprightly needles wave and twirl,
In a dance, they giggle and swirl.
Whispers tumble from the boughs,
A jester's hat where humor bows.

Breezes carry their jovial tease,
The trees laugh, oh what a breeze!
Accents of chuckles fill the light,
Nature's jesters, a pure delight.

Each leaf a grin, so full, so wide,
In this merry wood, joy can't hide.
With every rustle, it's plain to see,
Laughter's language, wild and free.

So come and dance beneath the green,
Where the sprightly sway is always seen.
Join the laughter, lose your weight,
In this joyful grove, celebrate.

## Laughter in the Luminescence

Amidst the glow of twilight's gleam,
A tree spills jokes like a funny dream.
Its luminescence brightens the night,
With laughter bouncing, pure delight.

Fireflies twinkle, mesmerized,
They jiggle around, pleasantly surprised.
Each crack of humor, a spark to ignite,
Moments of joy that feel just right.

The moon winks down, a witness to fun,
As the laughter warms everyone.
In this shining space where spirits roam,
Happy hearts feel right at home.

So gather 'round where the shadows play,
Let the light and laughter lead the way.
In this bright grove, take a chance,
Join the tree in a joyous dance.

# Melody of the Gentle Breeze

A gentle breeze plays a tune,
Through leafy branches, morning to noon.
It carries whispers, soft and light,
A melody of laughter, pure delight.

The rustling leaves, they join in song,
With nature's chorus, all day long.
Each note a tickle, each gust a grin,
Creating joy from deep within.

Tiny critters bounce, caught in the swing,
With every giggle, they start to sing.
In this orchestra of fun and cheer,
The world expands, drawing us near.

So listen close to the breezy hum,
Let the sweet notes make your heart thrum.
For in this laughter-filled embrace,
You'll find a magic in every space.

## Amusement in the Arboreal

In the grove where branches sway,
The trees share jokes in a playful way.
Bark and leaves are in on it too,
Tickling each other as the breezes blew.

Squirrels giggle, leaping high,
Flipping acorns like a circus sky.
Woodpeckers chuckle in their busy work,
While the bunnies hop, a joyful quirk.

The shadows dance to a comic tune,
As sunlight jests with the lazy moon.
Every rustle and whisper adds to the cheer,
Nature's laughter ringing loud and clear.

So if you wander beneath the green,
You'll find a comedy like none have seen.
Among the trunks and the leafy crowns,
Amusement abounds where fun knows no bounds.

## The Harmonious Haven

In the haven where the branches meet,
Laughter echoes with a rhythmic beat.
The foxes prance in a silly disguise,
With winks and nods and playful lies.

Chirps and chirrups fill the air,
As critters gather from everywhere.
A raccoon juggles under the light,
While owls hoot, guiding the night.

Dancing leaves twirl with glee,
Branching out like a big, happy family.
The breeze carries whispers of delight,
Making even the silence feel bright.

Every nook holds a quirky jest,
Nature's riddle, a playful quest.
In this sanctuary where laughter resounds,
Joy is the treasure that knows no bounds.

## Echoing Elation in Every Leaf

Amidst the foliage so lush and green,
Laughter bounces, a delightful scene.
Every leaf giggles, sways, and spins,
   Echoing joy that never gives in.

Twirling branches shake with glee,
A merry band, a jolly jubilee.
The flowers grin, their colors bright,
Throwing petals in sheer delight.

From the acorns' plop to the songbird's cheer,
Every sound tickles, bringing good cheer.
Mirth infects the air all around,
A harmonious symphony of joy profound.

As dusk wraps its arms, the stars ignite,
The trees chuckle softly, a comforting sight.
In this playful world, let worries cease,
Embrace the echoes, and find your peace.

## Playful Murmurs of the Wind

In the glade where whispers spin,
Trees giggle as the breezes grin.
Branches sway in light ballet,
Nature's jesters dance and play.

Bark embossed with silly lines,
Roots entwined in playful vines.
Leaves cascade like laughter's song,
Echoing where we belong.

Squirrels watch with curious eyes,
As the sunbeam gently flies.
Bouncing shadows on the ground,
Joyful pranks that know no bound.

With a flutter, they will spin,
Mirthful breezes pull us in.
In the light, we twirl and sing,
To the tale that nature brings.

## Joyful Roots and Branches

Roots beneath the surface tease,
Twisting tales among the breeze.
Branches stretch in playful arcs,
Fill the air with laughter's sparks.

In the forest, giggles bloom,
Sunlight weaves through leafy room.
Nature's jest, a silly game,
Whispers soft, but never tame.

Little critters dance around,
Chasing echoes, leaping sound.
Every rustle, every sound,
Joyful secrets abound.

With each chuckle in the air,
Hearts are light, and free of care.
In this realm of endless glee,
Nature's laughter sets us free.

## Swaying with Laughter

Underneath the golden light,
Trees are swaying, such a sight!
With a giggle, leaves will prance,
In the sun, they take a chance.

Branches bob with cheeky grace,
Nature's smile on every face.
Playful whispers, soft and bright,
Carry joy with pure delight.

Breezes swirl like tickled toes,
Chasing shadows where it goes.
Every twig a jester's wand,
Creation's laughter, bright and fond.

With the rustle and the sway,
Magic lives in lighthearted play.
In the woods, we find our dance,
A merry twist, a gleeful chance.

## Elysian Echoes of the Earth

Amidst the trunks, echoes ring,
Joyous sounds that nature brings.
With the rustling, leaves declare,
Laughter dances on the air.

In the twilight, shadows tease,
Whimsical among the trees.
Bark adorned with playful curves,
Holds the laughter that preserves.

As the night in silence hums,
Nature's choir softly strums.
Stars above seem to delight,
In the comedy of night.

With each tickle from the breeze,
Life unfolds with playful ease.
In this realm of joy we tread,
Where every sigh is laughter bred.

## Chortles in the Treetops

Up high in the trees, where the giggles soar,
The branches shake hands, they won't be a bore.
With whispers of joy, the leaves play along,
They dance in the breeze, a whimsical song.

A squirrel in a bowtie does a little spin,
While birds crack jokes, let the chuckles begin.
The sunbeams bounce in, tickling the bark,
In this forest of laughter, there's never a dark.

With acorns as maracas, they shake and they sway,
As nature's own circus, they laugh all day.
The shadows leap out, with the punchlines they toss,
In this joyful green space, there's never a loss.

So climb up a branch, join the raucous delight,
For humor is found where the hearts take flight.
In chortles of nature, let your worries depart,
In this playful tree haven, joy fills every heart.

**The Cheerful Arbor**

In the center of woods stands a jolly old tree,
With a trunk that can giggle, as happy as can be.
The branches they sway with a whimsical charm,
Bringing smiles to all in their leafy warm arm.

The birds tell tall tales, with feathers so bright,
And mischief runs wild as they flit in their flight.
With a rustle and chuckle, each critter will share,
The secrets of laughter that dance in the air.

Beneath its grand cover, where laughter can't cease,
The bees swing and buzz like they're bursting with glee.
And at every new tickle from the passing breeze,
The leaves burst with joy, like a faction of keys.

So come share the cheer where the funny things bloom,
In the heart of the wood where the wild spirits zoom.
Let the giggles surround you, wrap tight like a shawl,
In the cheerful old arbor, there's laughter for all.

## Rhapsody of the Forest Floor

Down low where the mushrooms sprout laughter so sweet,
The critters convene for a whimsical meet.
With giggles and snickers, the undergrowth thrives,
As the roots share the jokes where the humor arrives.

A hedgehog spins tales of his prickly old days,
While a fox taps his paws in a rhythmic ballet.
The dandelions puff, sending laughter to sky,
As the grasshoppers chirp, on a musical high.

With squeaks and soft grumbles, they echo with glee,
A party of fungi joins in harmony.
They jive with the beetles who twist and they twirl,
In this rhapsody bright, let the fun unfurl.

So stomp on the forest floor, dance with delight,
With nature's own chorus, we'll laugh through the night.
In this merry mosaic where shadows implore,
Join the rhapsody here on the wild forest floor.

## **Revelry in the Rustling Leaves**

In the canopy high, where the breezes hold sway,
There's splendor and joy in a lively display.
With rustles and tittering, the branches do play,
While laughter surrounds us, like games on the way.

A chipmunk with marbles rolls one down the path,
Each bump sends a giggle, igniting a laugh.
The wind tickles softly while branches applaud,
In the revelry here, let no spirits be flawed.

With twinkles of light dancing down through the green,
The joy in the leaves paints a whimsical scene.
From the tips of the ferns to the bark of the pine,
There's laughter in nature, a blessing divine.

So relish the moments where fun takes a seat,
In the rustling leaves, where the world feels complete.
Let the smiling branches sweep burdens away,
For laughter's the treasure we find every day.

www.ingramcontent.com/pod-product-compliance
Lightning Source LLC
Chambersburg PA
CBHW051701160426
43209CB00004B/980